MY MOMMY IS
A SCHOOLTEACHER

Nasra Noor

DIVERSE VOICES PRESS

My Mommy is a Schoolteacher
Text copyright 2023 by Nasra Noor
Illustration copyright 2023 by Victoria Medi

ISBN: 979-8-9868024-5-9
Library of Congress Control Number: 2023906108
Printed in the United States of America
First printing 2023

Production Manager: Hudda Ibrahim
Editor: Abdi Mahad
Cover and interior design: Victoria Medi

Diverse Voices Press
3333 W. Division St. Suite 112
Saint Cloud, MN 56301

(206) 446-5593
www.DiverseVoicesPress.com

To order, visit:
www.DiverseVoicesPress.com
Reseller discounts available.

This book belongs to

_____

Hooyo is always busy. She rises before the sunrise to juggle all her chores.

She takes care of us, makes canjeero,
and cleans with an incredible passion.

Each morning, she packs the lunches, hugs us, and prays for our safe return.

Hooyo drives us to school and after that to Dugsi. She shares some funny stories with us on the journey.

She tells us that we are her greatest treasure and her complete joy.

Her affection and friendship allow us to get through the good and bad days.

After dropping us off, she goes to the Halal store
and shops for what to eat for dinner.

During the day while we are at school, she cooks up bariis or baasto to serve with the evening meal.

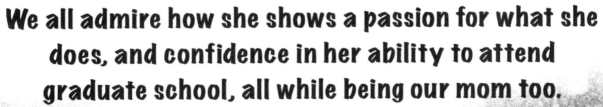

We all admire how she shows a passion for what she does, and confidence in her ability to attend graduate school, all while being our mom too.

When Hooyo is at school, Aabo tells folktale stories. Our oldest sister, Najma, helps with our homework. She's very smart and we admire her and look up to her. She's a blessing who fills our hearts with love and joy.

Aabo tells us stories that give us jitters, and make us roll on the floor with laughter. Some of the stories are about villains, some about fearless heroes and heroines, and others about goofy tricksters.

After we finish listening to the nail-biting stories, Aabo reads books to me and my sisters that lull us to sleep.

He tucks us in and says, "Goodnight."

Before I fall asleep every night, I silently thank Hooyo for everything she does for us.

I pray for her to stay strong and ask Almighty Allah to watch over her and keep her safe.

One morning, mom greets us with a
giant smile on her face.
"Next week I'm graduating", she says.

"Congrats," all of us say out loud as we jump for joy. Hooyo's big day has arrived!

When the day comes, we dress up fancy to attend the graduation ceremony.

On the way to the university auditorium, we stop at a
nearby store to buy cards and balloons for Hooyo.

In the backseat of our van, my siblings and I decorate cards to congratulate her.

With our van rolling down the road, I begin to think about Mom's fantastic traits, how wonderful, how strong, how caring, how patient, and how creative she is.

Whenever I'm down, she's always there for me, showing me how much she cares about me. I am grateful for her bringing me comfort and confidence.

At the auditorium, we all take our seats. All the families are hustling and bustling to their seats in stylish clothes. Our cousins, Abdullahi and Abdirahman, stand by our side.

Soon Hooyo's name is called. Me and
my siblings stand up next to Aabo
and cheer for her. She smiles at us
as she walks across the stage.

When the diploma is being handed to her,
we all clap till our palms hurt.
Tears of joy drop out of my eyes.
It was a moment to remember, a moment to cherish.
Thanks to her hard work and dedication, a milestone
was achieved and finally crowned.

Ever since the day mom graduated, hope has been blooming inside me. I tell myself if mom can do it all, I can do it too!

Every time people ask me what my mom does, I look them straight in the eye and proudly say, "My Mom is a teacher."

GLOSSARY OF SOMALI TERMS

AABO　　　　　Father

BAASTO　　　　Pasta

BARIIS　　　　Rice

CANJEERO　　　Injero - Sourdough flatbread

DUGSI　　　　 Islamic school

HALAL STORE　 Halal store is a store that sells any food that accepts Islamic law and is typically consumed by practicing Muslims

HOOYO　　　　 Mother